SkillBites

Get wiser in 10 minutes

THE ESSENTIALS OF

NEGOTIATING EFFECTIVELY

Judy Weintraub

Weintraub Legal Services

Discover other titles by Judy Weintraub at SkillBites.net:

How to Build Successful Business Partnerships

TABLE OF CONTENTS

INTRODUCTION

Most people dislike negotiations. This may stem from fear that they won't get what they want, or that their requests will be rejected, or that they will appear weak.

Negotiating effectively, however, is based in large part on your state of mind. If you go into a negotiation with confidence, you are more likely to achieve your objectives.

If you are timid in your approach or demeanor, you will probably be taken advantage of. This book contains some valuable tips to provide you with greater assurance when you negotiate, which will improve your negotiating effectiveness. In particular, the book covers the following topics:

1. Preparing for a negotiation;

2. Finding opportunities to practice negotiating;

3. Delivering an effective opening proposal;

4. Building rapport and trust;

5. Conducting the negotiations;

6. Dealing with tactics and difficult behaviors;

7. Responding to common rejections;

8. Making concessions;

9. Addressing gender and cultural differences; and

10. Documenting the results

PREPARING FOR A NEGOTIATION

Good preparation is critical to being able to achieve your objectives in a negotiation. Preparation consists of 3 main steps:

✓ Gathering information,

✓ Identifying your options, and

✓ Developing and practicing your proposal.

Each of these will be addressed in turn.

a. Gathering Information

The more important the negotiations, the more time you will want to spend at this stage. Some of the information you will want to gather or think about includes the following:

- Your goals: What do you want to achieve in the negotiations? Why is this important to you? Why would it be fair for the other side to give this to you?

- The other side's position: What do you think the other side wants? What objections do you think they might have to giving you what you want?

- Your leverage: What do you have that they might want? What is their leverage?

- The other negotiator: Who will be negotiating on behalf of the other side? What is their negotiating style? What is their background?

- Others impacted: Is there anyone else who might be impacted by the negotiation? If so, should you obtain their input?

- External Factors: Are there any external factors you need to consider, such as industry standards, economic conditions or possibly currency fluctuations?

b. Identifying Options

Rarely is there only one acceptable outcome in a negotiation. Try to think of as many different desirable outcomes as possible. You may find that there are several options that are beneficial for you, which gives you a greater likelihood of getting a good outcome in the negotiation.

For instance, if you are buying a new car, the price is certainly one factor, but there are several other options that could have significant value for you, such as a discount on some desirable accessories, or a longer warranty period, or free oil changes, or free loaners when your car needs maintenance.

If you are trying to negotiate a salary increase, some other options might include:

- A review in 6 months with a salary increase if you meet a specified set of goals,

- Stock options,

- A higher title,

- Payment for training,

- Flex time, or

- More vacation time.

Once you have identified the options, you should prioritize them based on their value to you. What would be the best outcome? What is realistic? What would be the minimum you would accept before walking away? You should also consider what your alternatives are if the negotiation fails.

Then consider the options you have come up with from the perspective of the other side. What do you think their objections might be, and how will you address those objections? What might their options be that they may ask you for, and what would be your response to their request?

Going through this exercise will broaden your perspective and give you greater flexibility in the negotiations, in the event that the other side cannot or will not accept your best case scenario.

c. Developing and practicing your proposal

Many people start with a weak offer to avoid rejection. To get what you want, you should develop your proposal around your optimal solution. While you may not get everything you want, you will get a better result than by starting with a weak proposal. Be aware, however, that if you start with a position that is so extensive that it could be viewed as unreasonable, you might jeopardize the whole negotiation.

After you identify what you want, you then want to explain why it is fair and reasonable. Include how your proposal might meet the other side's interests. Anticipate any objections they might have and address those as well. Addressing objections prior to the other side raising them tends to deflate the objections.

How you present your proposal plays a major role in whether it is accepted. A demand is more likely to be rejected even if it meets the other side's needs. Posture, tone of voice and other non-verbal signals that you consciously or unconsciously transmit are important – make sure to sit up, not slouched. Practice giving your proposal so that it sounds smooth, but not too rehearsed. Your voice should project to reflect confidence, and not drop at the end of sentences.

Get feedback from others as to both the substance and the tone of your delivery. Were they persuaded by your presentation? Did they feel you came across as sincere, confident and credible? Ask them to take on the role of the person you are going to be negotiating against. If you can respond to hard questions from them, you should be prepared to respond to most issues that could come up during the negotiation.

PRACTICE YOUR
NEGOTIATING SKILLS

Most people have trouble asking for what they want. If you have this difficulty, try practicing your negotiation skills in small, unimportant transactions where it doesn't matter if you don't get what you are asking for. There are lots of opportunities to practice: if you are going on vacation or on a business trip, ask your hotel for a discount, or a higher class room. If you are renewing a newspaper or magazine subscription, ask for a discount. If you get a credit card statement in the mail showing a finance charge for late payment, call and ask for the charge to be waived. You might have to wait on hold for 15 minutes, but you can be doing something else while waiting. Many credit card companies routinely waive those charges when the customer asks (so long as you don't do this very often).

When you are buying something, ask for a discount, or free shipping, or a longer warranty or something else of value. If you get turned down, you can decide whether you want to pursue it further, perhaps by asking for the person's manager, or just accept their response and move on. Think of it as a training exercise, so you don't feel bad getting rejected. In any event, you don't really lose anything if your request gets turned down, as the result is the same as if you hadn't asked. But unless you ask, you won't get anything better. And the more you practice asking, the more comfortable you will become, which will stand you in good stead when you have to negotiate something important.

Here is an example of a practice opportunity:

Judy and Bruce were driving through Switzerland. At 7 pm, they came to a lovely hotel on Lake Lucerne, and sought to stay there. Judy went in while Bruce stayed in the car. Upon inquiring, she was told there were several rooms available. When advised of the room rate, Judy "flinched", thanked the receptionist, but regretfully declined because the rate was out of their budget range. The receptionist then offered to lower the rate by roughly $50, but Judy responded that her husband was probably not willing to spend that much either. The receptionist then asked whether lowering the rate another $50 would be acceptable to her husband. "That does include breakfast, does it not?" asked Judy. After a *brief pause, the receptionist responded affirmatively, to which Judy advised that the rate would be acceptable.*

This example shows several negotiating tactics:

- ✓ **Flinching** can be a useful response, as it implies that an offer is unacceptable without saying anything.

- ✓ Relying on a **higher authority**, in this case Judy's husband, can also be beneficial; you can place the blame on someone else for turning down their offer. But if the other side tries this on you, you will want to ask them to have the other person present, so as not to be negotiating with a middle man.

- ✓ Asking about the inclusion of breakfast, sometimes referred to as **nibbling**, can get you a little more value; but again be careful if the other side tries this on you. It can be frustrating if you are on the receiving end, and can re-open what appeared to be a done deal.

- ✓ Finally, think of your **leverage**. In this case, Judy knew that at 7 pm the hotel wasn't likely to get a lot of people coming to stay the night, so she had leverage over the hotel, which would be better off renting a room at a substantial discount than getting nothing.

Could she have done better? Possibly, but the objective is not to get every last penny. Knowing in advance what they were willing to spend on a hotel room meant that Judy was satisfied in accepting the rate when it fell into their range. Looking at the alternatives, at 7 pm, Judy and Bruce didn't want to continue looking for a hotel.

OPENING PROPOSAL

There is an advantage to going first in a negotiation. The first offer sets the bar or "anchors" the parties' expectations. It also sets the tone for the negotiations, and a well presented offer demonstrates the competency of the presenter.

As previously mentioned, you should build your opening proposal around your most desired result, as long as you can explain why your request is reasonable. Address the other side's needs or interests as well as any objections you anticipate they might have. Use a reasonable and respectful tone and you will likely find that their response will in turn be reasonable and respectful.

If you are really nervous, take some slow deep breaths, speak slowly, smile, make eye contact, and take a sip or two of water. These tips will make you appear confident to the other side, even when you don't feel confident. It is the other side's perception of your confidence that is more important for negotiating effectively than any actual confidence (or lack thereof) that you feel.

If you really don't feel prepared to present first, you can start by asking questions designed to elicit information, such as their needs and interests, and work on developing rapport (discussed further in the next chapter). Some people are reluctant to go first in case they ask for too little. However, if your offer meets your needs, then you shouldn't worry whether you might have been able to get more.

If you go first and then after they make their proposal you learn something that changes what you are willing to offer, you can tell the person that you were unaware of that information, you would like to take a break and think about what you've just learned, and you may need to revise your proposal as a result of the new information.

BUILD RAPPORT AND TRUST

When you build rapport and trust with the party with whom you are negotiating, the negotiations are much more likely to be amicable, and each side will achieve a satisfactory result. Two ways to build rapport and trust are making a connection with the other party and using their own style. As part of your preparation, you should try to learn as much as possible about the other party and try to identify something you both have in common. Perhaps you grew up in the same neighborhood, have kids the same age, like playing the same sport or have mutual friends. When you share something in common, you gain credibility and they are more likely to listen to you.

By using similar behaviors or style as the other person, you can increase their comfort in the negotiation. To discern their style, listen to the words they use. If they use visual language, such as "I **see** your point," then use similar language. If they use auditory language, such as "I **hear** you," or kinesthetic language, "I **feel** that you don't understand," then use that language. You can also watch their eyes. If they look up when thinking, they are more likely to be visual thinkers. If they look to the side, they are auditory processors and if they look down, they are kinesthetic processors.

Similarly, observe how they present their proposal and how they approach decisions. For instance, if they use a lot of data, then provide data concerning your proposal. If they express a lot of emotion, then providing a lot of data is likely to be a turn off.

Observe their body language and "mirror" their posture. If they cross their arms, then you can do the same or something similar. Following these simple techniques will help you build rapport, which will enable you to accomplish more of your goals in the negotiation.

CONDUCTING THE NEGOTIATIONS

When possible, try to arrange for the negotiations to be held face-to-face. You are able to discern a lot more information from body language and tone, than if you are negotiating over the phone or even in a video conference.

Observe the other person. Do they appear to be listening, or are they distracted?

Do they seem anxious, frustrated, mad, or sad? You can address their emotions once you have identified their emotional state.

Listen carefully to what they are saying, and do your best not to interrupt. This shows respect, and increases the likelihood that they will listen carefully to you when you talk. Moreover, you may learn some important information that you weren't previously aware of, such as a critical interest or need of theirs. If they seem particularly emotional about something or are repeating something, that is a strong indication that the point they are making is important to them. If you can't figure out what their interest is, you can ask. "This seems like it is very important to you. Can you help me understand why you need that?"

Try to remain cool headed. If you find yourself getting angry or frustrated, ask for a break. When we get emotional, we tend to say things we shouldn't, we lose focus and objectivity, we become defensive and we shut down our ability to think of alternatives, all of which are detrimental to achieving our objectives. And if you find that the other side is getting overly emotional or frustrated, you might suggest a break to help them calm down.

Be polite, professional and cooperative. When you exhibit these behaviors, it reduces tensions, shows respect and tends to engender similar conduct from the other side, which makes the negotiations much more pleasant. This is particularly important when the relationship is ongoing.

Be creative. Try to think of the negotiation as a problem to be solved: you need XYZ, they need ABC, so what can be done to meet everyone's needs? When you encourage this approach, you get the other side working with you, rather than at cross purposes.

More on Listening. Listening is such an important part of effective negotiations that it is worth delving a little deeper into effective listening skills. One of the hard parts about listening is turning off the voice in our heads that is reacting to what is being said. It is like trying to listen to two conversations at the same time. Try not to react to what is being said, but merely take it in. If it helps, take notes, as that will keep your focus on what is being said. If you have a question about what is being said, write it down. Try not to interrupt. If you find that you are losing attention, ask to take a break.

You can show that you are listening attentively by leaning forward, nodding your head or saying "ah huh" every now and then, and asking questions when the person is finished speaking. Make sure you are also "listening" to the non-verbal communications – the person's posture, dress, eyes, tone, rate of speech, volume, facial expressions, and body language. Studies have shown that only about 7% of our message is derived from the words we use.

As you are listening, try to identify what the other side's needs and interests are. Seek confirmation that you have understood their position or identified their interests correctly: "Let me make sure I understand what you are saying. If I hear you correctly, I gather you are looking for ..." Not only will you confirm your understanding, but you will convey that you have been listening attentively to what they have been saying.

DEALING WITH TACTICS AND DIFFICULT BEHAVIORS

There are many types of tactics used in negotiations, usually designed to create tension, intimidate the other side, distract them from their issues or get them to make a hasty decision. Below are some strategies for dealing with tactics or behaviors that may cause problems for you.

1. **Stay calm.** The first step is not to react. Resist the urge to respond in kind. Be cognizant of your own emotions, so when you feel yourself becoming emotional, take some deep breaths and try to figure out what has caused the emotions. Think of the other person's behavior as tactic, which will help diffuse your emotions. Try not to take objections personally.

2. **Focus on interests.** Many times people resort to tactics because they feel they haven't been understood. Try acknowledging their interests, or ask them to explain their interests. Employ

the techniques discussed above regarding active listening and building rapport and trust.

3. **Find common ground.** Try to find areas of agreement. If the other side is feeling frustrated by the slow progress, recap the progress that has been made. Ask them for ideas as to how to move forward more productively.

4. **Change the situation.** Change the people at the table, the venue or even the issue being addressed. Take a break, whether for 10 minutes or a few days. Let people cool down and re-focus.

5. **Give a gift.** Take the person out to lunch, or pay for lunch to be brought in, or bring some candy to your next meeting. When you give a gift like this, it reduces tension and opens people's minds, enabling them to see you as a person and not an enemy. There is great power in "breaking bread" together.

6. **Leave.** As a last resort, walk away. Don't use this unless you are fully prepared to end the negotiations. If you come back to the table when they don't respond, you will lose all credibility. But leave the door open – tell the other side that you are willing to continue the negotiations if they are prepared to move forward on the issue over which you are deadlocked.

COMMON REJECTIONS

You can expect to get rejections in negotiations. Know that you don't have to accept them. Try not to take them personally, and try to identify the underlying interest being jeopardized that has led to the rejection. Here are some common forms of rejection and some suggested responses.

"Take it or leave it"

Response: "Are you saying you don't have authority to do anything different? Is there someone else I should talk to?" If you believe it would not be in the other side's interest to have you "leave it," point out how that would not be in either side's best interest. Offer some other alternative that could meet their needs and allow them to save face.

"It's company policy"

Response: "Company policies are generally devised to protect the company against certain circumstances. Can you tell me what the interest is behind the policy? Can we figure out a different way to protect your company's interest?"

"Your price is too high"

Response: Address the value of your proposition, and how your proposal meets their needs in ways that they might not have fully appreciated. Explore their interests further – is there anything you could take out of the package to reduce the price that they don't really need? Would setting up a payment plan help? Perhaps offer a larger quantity for a longer term, qualifying them for a quantity discount.

CONCESSIONS AND NIBBLING

Most people feel compelled to offer a concession somewhat comparable to what the other side has offered. There is no rule that says you must do so. Similarly, if you offer a concession to the other side, don't expect that they will come back with something comparable.

Keep in mind that any concession indicates that more concessions will be made by that party. Large concessions indicate that there is a lot more that can be conceded, while small concessions give the impression that the bottom line is not far off. Never feel obligated to split the difference. That is one option, but may not meet your needs.

If the other side asks for something after you have reached a deal, even if it is acceptable to you, try to figure out something you can ask for. This will discourage them for asking for other things, and may get you something more than you would otherwise have obtained.

For example, you've just completed a negotiation, and the other side comes back and says "oh, we need to spread out the payments over 2 years instead of one year." You could agree, provided that they pay interest of, say, 6% on the unpaid amount; or you could ask for something else unrelated to what they asked for that they had turned down, or something that was never discussed (perhaps the right to issue a press release announcing the deal, or a commitment on their part to give you an endorsement that you could use in your marketing materials).

GENDER AND CULTURAL DIFFERENCES

Understanding people's negotiating style can help you chart a course to achieve greater results in negotiations. While there are many exceptions, there are certain gender-based styles to keep in mind. When doing your pre-negotiation preparation, or as you observe the other person during the negotiations, try to discern whether they are exhibiting gender stereotypical behavior.

Women are generally interested in not jeopardizing a relationship. They tend to be less direct, and more "touchy-feely." When negotiating against women, plan to spend more time building the relationship.

Men tend to view negotiations more as a competition: one person will win and the other will lose. They take harder positions, are more direct and prefer to stick to facts. When negotiating against men, spend time sharing your credentials, and be prepared with data to back your position.

When negotiating with someone who may come from a different background, try to learn about the customs of the other person's culture. In some countries, such as Japan, for instance, it is rude to negotiate before developing a relationship. If you rush the negotiations, you risk losing the deal. Some cultures view time very differently from our Western culture. Here, it is rude to be late to a meeting; in France, on the other hand, being on time is not a priority. Asians tend not to like touching, while Italians stand very close and engage in a lot of touching. Americans generally distrust people who don't make eye contact, while in Japan, it is viewed as disrespectful to make eye contact with a superior. Ignorance of another's culture could greatly hinder your negotiations.

DOCUMENTING THE RESULTS

Even if you haven't completed the negotiations at the end of a negotiation session, and are planning to resume another time, it is important to document what you have accomplished. It is amazing how people in the same meeting can have very different recollections a few days later. Documenting the results can avoid memory differences.

Often, in the process of documenting the discussion, other issues come up. Don't be chagrined. If they didn't come up, they might cause a monkey wrench in the relationship later. This way, they can get addressed appropriately.

What to document: Some of the important items to include in your documentation include the following:

- ✓ Identify who attended the negotiation, and where and when it took place.
- ✓ Describe what issues were addressed. For those issues that were resolved, identify what was the resolution. For those that weren't

resolved, identify what was the last offer on the table for each party.

✓ Identify any action items or next steps, who is supposed to do what, by when, and, depending on how important the follow-up is, what happens if the action isn't taken in a timely manner.

After each person has had an opportunity to review what has been documented, get their signature *before they leave the meeting*. A weaker alternative, if you aren't able to get this, is to send a follow-up confirmation that the documentation represents an accurate summary of the negotiation. Make sure you also follow up on any action items. Otherwise, the benefit of the negotiation might be substantially lost.

SUMMARY

You can improve your negotiating effectiveness by following these tips:

1. Prepare for negotiations by gathering information, identifying and evaluating options and practicing the delivery of your presentation.

2. Practice your negotiating skills in unimportant situations to give you more confidence.

3. Go first in presenting your proposal, if you are prepared, to "anchor" the expectations.

4. Build rapport and trust by making connections and utilizing the other person's style.

5. During the negotiations, listen attentively, both to words and body language, stay calm and be respectful.

6. If the negotiations get heated, try these strategies: detach yourself and stay calm; identify what interest is being jeopardized; change the situation; offer something; or walk away, as a last resort.

7. Don't feel compelled to give comparable concessions, or split the difference, or accept any "nibbling."

8. Don't accept a rejection without further exploration.

9. Learn about the person's negotiating style and any cultural issues before commencing the negotiation, and plan accordingly.

10. Document the results of the negotiation, even if not completed, and get sign off.

Remember that every negotiation involves give and take. Try not to dwell on what you didn't get, but be satisfied that you each got a better result than had the negotiation failed.

ABOUT THE AUTHOR

Judy Weintraub is an attorney with over 30 years legal experience. She has served as corporate counsel and as an executive in senior management at a multi-billion dollar company where she was the chief negotiator on major procurements. She is a serial entrepreneur, with four successful businesses: Weintraub Legal Services, providing corporate legal services to businesses in the mid-Atlantic region; ACCORD, LLC, offering mediation and arbitration services; ABLR, co-founded with Harrie Samaras, providing training and consulting in dispute resolution; and most recently, SkillBites, providing book writing and publishing services to entrepreneurs and professionals to enable them to accelerate their growth.

Judy can be reached at 610-783-4519 or judy@weintraublegal.com.

Discover other titles by Judy Weintraub at SkillBites.net: *How to Build Successful Business Partnerships*